THE COLORADO COLLEGE STUDIES

Editor

Timothy Fuller

ISRAELI LITERATURE: A CASE OF REALITY REFLECTING FICTION

Amos Oz

The William Jovanovich Lecture
at
Colorado College
February 6, 1985

THE COLORADO COLLEGE STUDIES, NUMBER TWENTY-ONE, 1985
THE COLORADO COLLEGE, COLORADO SPRINGS

The Colorado College Studies
The Colorado College, Colorado Springs
Colorado 80903

Copyright 1985 by The Colorado College
All rights reserved

The Colorado College Studies Issue No. 21
Published in the United States of America
ISBN: 0-935052-12-7
Library of Congress Catalogue Card Number: 85-70645

ISRAELI LITERATURE: A CASE OF REALITY REFLECTING FICTION

Amos Oz

Introduction

It is a pleasure to welcome you to what has become one of the most anticipated events of the year at Colorado College, the annual William Jovanovich Lecture in Public Affairs. This lecture has enhanced the intellectual life of the campus by making it possible for us to bring here people who have made significant contributions in many different fields, people with exacting minds capable of elucidating complex issues. Daniel Boorstin, the Librarian of Congress, delivered the first Jovanovich Lecture in 1978. And those who have followed have been equally distinguished — Chaim Herzog, the former ambassador of Israel to the United Nations; Norman Podhoretz, editor of *Commentary*; Eugene McCarthy, the presidential candidate and outspoken senator from Minnesota; the Canadian environmentalist and diplomat, Maurice Strong. And this year, the widely acclaimed novelist from Israel: Amos Oz.

This Lecture was established in 1978 by a friend of the College to honor William Jovanovich, a Coloradan, a writer, an editor and a publisher of distinction. In the words of then-President Lloyd Worner, the Lecture Series was "to pay honor to a great American literary figure and to provide for clarification of major public issues of the past, present and future." It is particularly fitting that a lecture of this sort should have been established in Mr. Jovanovich's honor because he is a man interested in exploring ideas and in furthering education.

It is also particularly fitting, and for us, particularly fortunate, that this year Amos Oz is delivering the Jovanovich Lecture, because in addition to being one of the most important writers published by Harcourt, Brace, Jovanovich, Mr. Oz is at Colorado College through Mr. Jovanovich's assistance. When, last year, Amos Oz expressed a desire to spend a year in the United States teaching and writing, it was Mr. Jovanovich who suggested that Colorado College might fill the bill. We are all extremely grateful for that suggestion, for it has brought to our midst Amos and Nily Oz, who have enriched our lives immeasurably.

So, this year's Jovanovich Lecture serves a new purpose, not to bring someone to our campus, but to provide a forum for a distinguished visitor we have been fortunate enough to have with us for this entire academic year.

Amos Oz has lived all his life in Israel and his writing is intimately connected to that country — to its trials, tribulations, successes, struggles and evolution. He was born in a suburb of Jerusalem during the time of the British Mandate, and lived there until 1954 when he joined Kibbutz Hulda where he still lives, works and teaches. He has published five novels, a book of short stories, two volumes of novellas, a children's book, and most recently a nonfiction work, *In the Land of Israel*, a book which I found to be a fascinating study of the polarities which define much of contemporary Israel: Faith and Certainty; Hitler and the Messiah; Israelis and Jews; Jews and Oriental Jews; Good and Evil; Jews and the Arabs. Amos Oz' books are read and praised in 15 countries and have been translated into almost as many languages.

While at Colorado College, he has been working on a new novel, supervising the translation of yet another, and has been teaching three courses, two in the English department and one in the political science department. Teaching, although not his profession, is not new to him. He still teaches in his kibbutz school; has been a fellow at St. Cross College, Oxford, where he was awarded a master of arts degree in 1970; has been a writer-in-residence at the Hebrew University in Jerusalem; has taught at Berkeley and has lectured at many American colleges and universities.

Amos Oz has been intensely involved with the political life of his country as a soldier, a journalist, and a spokesman for Peace Now, an anti-war, but nonpacifist, group he helped found in 1977, which is seeking a workable accommodation with the Arabs. He speaks eloquently for a rational and humane solution from a part of the world where fanaticism is familiar and hysteria often the norm. Perhaps because he has seen firsthand a series of wars in which he has participated, he is suspicious of the fanatic and the extremist. He has lived in Israel throughout all of its trials and tribulations and lived through its coming of age. He has seen the country evolve along with its language and literature.

It seems extraordinary that a country no bigger than the state of New Jersey, which has been fighting for its life ever since its birth, has somehow managed to create a body of literature that is read and respected throughout the world. The fact that such a literature exists is due in no small part to the efforts and to the talent of Amos Oz. He has chosen tonight to speak about that writing: "Israeli Literature: A Case of Reality Reflecting Fiction". Ladies and gentlemen: Amos Oz.

Gresham Riley, President
Colorado College
February 6, 1985

Preface

Allow me to begin with a personal remark: I feel deeply grateful to Colorado College for very many things, not least among them being this opportunity to pay tribute to my unique American publisher, William Jovanovich.

Mr. Jovanovich, as you ought to know, is an extremely dangerous man: under his guidance and leadership, Harcourt, Brace, Jovanovich has been, for many years, a major channel for the infiltration and penetration of America by various foreign literatures. Along with Helen Wolff, the greatest living literary editor in this country, and her enthusiastic successor at Harcourt, Brace, Jovanovich, Drenka Willen, Mr. Jovanovich has conducted and orchestrated a vivacious publishing realm. Indeed, he has acted as a secret agent for the invasion, in some cases even the conquest, of America by a mixed multitude of various foreign powers, turning Harcourt, Brace, Jovanovich into what I believe is the most pluralistic and polyphonic publishing house in this country.

I am proud to be a modest part of Mr. Jovanovich's invading troops, a role which I intend to try to fulfill in what follows by pouring on you a very esoteric tale: Some of the saga of modern Hebrew Literature.

Amos Oz

Israeli Literature: A Case of Reality Reflecting Fiction

Ladies and gentlemen, shalom to all of you. My intention is to tell you one or two things about contemporary Hebrew literature, but as a matter of fact, I have second thoughts about the subject of this talk. It's the word "contemporary" which baffles me. It occurs to me, really, that I should tell you some of the story of modern Hebrew literature, rather than pretend to sum it up for you and to squeeze it into definitions and formulae: I am a storyteller, not a scholar. Now, stories are never "contemporary"; not even if they are set in the present time, not even when they are told in the present tense. A story is bound, almost by definition, to relate to the past. Storytellers are cripples, monsters really, born with their necks and faces turned backwards.

Of course, we all know of poets and storytellers who have had amazing revelations about the future, verging sometimes on the prophetic, writers who foresaw way ahead of ideologists and politicians (not that I regard being ahead of politicians such a big deal). But even those writers who had this "infrared" capacity for piercing the darkness of the future and for reading fortunes in advance, like Dostoievsky or Kafka, for example, even they were monsters with turned-back necks and faces. It was only through some mysterious looking-glass which they found somewhere in the past that they were able to peep into some of what was yet to come.

So you may expect to get tonight a report about the present, hoping perhaps to get by the same token even a glimpse of the future of Israel and its literature. And here I am, going to sell you nothing but old hats. I'm sorry.

But just how far into the past do I go? Where does my story properly begin?

The easiest thing to do is just to tell you about a number of significant recent Hebrew books, and then perhaps to give you some plot summaries. And then put it all in a context familiar to you: call this and that "expressionist", "existentialist", "political", and so on. You may even want me to tell you who exactly is Israel's Saul Bellow, who is Garcia Marquez, who resembles Gunther Grass, who are the Frosts, the Ted Hugheses or the Solzhenytsins in our little Israeli village. I admit that this is a tempting way. It could be fun. In fact, I sometimes tend to amuse people who are just faintly familiar with Israel's literary scene by telling them that this scene is much like that of a continuing earthquake, with various geological strata exposed to be watched simultaneously; if you hit the right cafe in Tel Aviv at the right time of the day you could see — at least until a few years ago — the John Donne of Hebrew poetry and the Lord Byron of Hebrew poetry, and the Walt Whitman and the T.S. Eliot sitting together at the same table with the local Allen Ginsberg, all of them alive (and kicking hard), all of them on speaking terms, or rather on screaming terms with each other. This situation is a result of the fact that literary developments which occurred in English and in other European literary traditions over centuries, took place within decades in Hebrew.

I could go even farther along the same line by telling you that modern Hebrew has several things in common with Elizabethan English: our language is still like melting lava, an erupting volcano; it's bubbling still with steam and with fumes and with fury. A poet or a writer of modern Hebrew is still in a position to "legislate" within the language; to force or seduce the language into "having it his or her way." I dare say that by comparison, modern English is a respectable elderly person with whom you do not dare take wild liberties so easily. (Admittedly Faulkner and Joyce and some other raving poets did just that to English, and did it all the way.)

But Hebrew nevertheless seems to encourage such practices: She still is a character of easy virtue.

Incidentally, by comparing modern Hebrew to Elizabethan English I'm not suggesting, of course, that each and every contemporary Hebrew writer is a William Shakespeare — of those we hardly have half a dozen!

But perhaps I'm making the wrong point altogether — the easier one. Because the truth is that despite some striking similarities, and despite strong influences from East and West European literatures, the basic context of Hebrew literature has always been Hebrew; and Jewish; and recently, Zionist. Which makes my task today much harder than it could have been if I thought that the context was basically European. As I said, modern Hebrew literature happens to be, in my view, much more than just an extension, a replica or a "province" of other literatures with which you may be more familiar.

Well, you see in fact I have been talking already for about five or ten minutes now, and I still don't know where and with what I am to begin my story. Which is perhaps a typical storyteller's syndrome, or a typical storyteller's dilemma: where does a story really begin? There is always a beginning before the beginning; an introduction to the prologue; or a birth before birth.

So just how far back should I go? "Had we but world enough and time. . ." I would have gone all the way back and followed the roots; back to the Bible. Back to the Mishna and Gemara and the prayers, and back to the fascinating appearance of the seemingly secular Hebrew literature in the heart of the Middle Ages in Spain and in other countries. I should have examined with you the revival of Hebrew drama and poetry and prose in the 18th and 19th centuries, a long time before the actual Renaissance of spoken Hebrew, which only took place a few decades ago and which has not yet been completed; because all of it is relevant and essential for the understanding of even the latest Hebrew poem, play, or novel, even those which only appeared the other day. Could anyone seriously discuss, say, T.S. Eliot without referring one way or another to Chaucer and Donne and Whitman? Or study Garcia Marquez without ever reading Cervantes? Or comment on Camus without even hearing of Flaubert and Stendahl? Strangely enough, some contemporary Israeli poets and novelists have been, in the last few years, exceedingly lucky and at the same time extremely unfortunate; they have traveled into many languages, they are relatively well-known in the literary world, but almost their entire context remains way behind. Amihai, for example, is read by many outside Israel, while Bialik and Steinberg and Vogel and Altermann did not travel that far, if at all. It is not that I am acting here as a travel agent, persuading you to invite, so to speak, those dead poets to join Amihai's journey. No, I am suggesting that this situation is unfair even to Amihai himself. Or take my own works: they are translated into several languages. Often I read about myself that I am some kind of little illegitimate offspring of some great French or Russian writer or another. Yet my legitimate literary mentors and parents, Berdichevsky, Brenner, Agnon, are relatively unknown to my readers outside Israel. Hence my urge to try and describe to you at least some of the Hebrew literary scene.

Had we but world enough and time.

So where, at last, do I begin my story? Perhaps I could start with the madmen: talk about the desperados — those Hebrew poets and writers who emerged from the ghettos of Eastern Europe at the turn of this century: Mendele and Berdichevsky, Bialik and Brenner and Gnessin — figures of "The Great Generation". I refer to them as madmen and desperados because they were writing in Hebrew for a hardly existing audience, with hardly any hopes for future generations of readers. For many years they wrote in Hebrew to be read mainly by their fellow Hebrew writers and by very few others. Some of them died without ever dreaming that their words would be taught in schools, that streets and kibbutzim would be named after them, or that they would get even so far as having their names mentioned today, here in this lovely town of Colorado Springs, Colorado.

In fact, at least some of them felt that they were the very end of Hebrew. They regarded themselves — at least some of them did — as authors of a tragic epilogue for an ancient drama which had opened millennia earlier and which was now, as they saw it, dying in the gutters.

So why didn't they simply quit? They were, after all, excellent writers. All of them could easily write in Yiddish, which at the time was still the language of millions and which, incidentally, was the native tongue of them all. Some of them could have gone very far in this world by switching to Russian, or German, with which they were at home. Who, at the turn of the century, really cared to read Hebrew? Whom did they have in mind?

I have to admit that to me it is still a fascinating mystery.

Actually, rather than solve it, I'm going to further complicate it: Bialik and Brenner and Berdichevsky and the others knew only too well that there were millions of Jews in the world at the turn of this century who could read Hebrew but would only read it in their holy books, and not — Heaven forbid! Perish the thought! — in secular books. While at the same time there were already more and more Jews ready and eager to read stories and poems, but would rather read them in Russian or German or Polish. So for whom did those members of "The Great Generation" write their Hebrew, whom did they have in mind?

All this is extremely relevant to our subject, as I happen to believe that at least a touch of the very same madness and of the very same despair is still there in every significant contemporary Hebrew work; just as it is still secretly feeding the true Zionism (not the distorted one though: I refer to despair and to zeal as opposed to insanity and fanaticism).

But let me get back to the point: where on earth do I begin my story? With Smolenskin perhaps, or with Mendele, who struggled to compose mimetic Hebrew prose a la Charles Dickens or a la Balzac and Victor Hugo, many years before any man in the world had ever said to a woman, "I love you," in modern Hebrew? (By the way, our problems in writing mimetic Hebrew prose nowadays are not as far from theirs as one might have thought.)

Or do I start with Bialik, who loved and who hated and demolished, and who at the same time preserved and reconstructed *in his Hebrew verse*, a Jewish world which in his days was still alive (in Yiddish) and still creative and vivacious (in Yiddish) and still blossoming (in Yiddish) with its last pulses of vigor? Why did Bialik and how could he, along with all the others, try to preserve this Yiddish world in Hebrew? Oh, those sons and lovers and killers and undertakers and monument builders and museum keepers of the great shadow-state of the Jews in Eastern Europe — why and how did they do all this in Hebrew rather than in Yiddish? Or, for that matter, rather than in Russian or German or Polish? After all, those writers, as well as their heroes, used to laugh and to weep and talk and dream and make love in languages other than Hebrew, which at the time was almost as dead as ancient Greek or Latin. Still, they make their Yiddish or Russian-speaking characters talk and curse and weep and make love in Hebrew. Why on earth did they do it?

I have my guess: there must have been some deep sense of despair beyond all this. And a terrible premonition of doom. Maybe they sensed somehow that all was lost anyway, that soon there would be no more Jews, no more Yiddish or Hebrew; maybe something in them wanted to close the circle with biblical passion and anger for which the Yiddish language was just too soft and cozy, whereas Russian or German would have been improper. Perhaps it really was like a homecoming of a dying man. At least of Bialik, Berdichevsky, and Brenner, I daresay that sometimes they wrote not for the living, not for any future generations or readers, but precisely for the ancient dead. Or was there, after all, some secret hope beyond hope? I do not know. All I know is that all of us write or talk to the dead in moments of great despair.

So where does my story begin? Maybe right at Number 48 Mile End Road, Whitechapel, London, in the year 1906, with 26-year-old Yosef Hayim Brenner who lived there, a wretched Jewish refugee from Russia, in a miserable rented room. He worked as a typesetter and lived on cabbage and potatoes, yet he was putting together nothing less than a fresh and modern and non-conformist Hebrew literary magazine. He printed it with his own hands and bound it with cheap glue and carried it in a sack on his back to the Post Office to be mailed to his 212 subscribers, scattered in eight or nine countries (hardly half a dozen of them in London itself), just a bunch of lunatics like himself who had not abandoned Hebrew, but were nonetheless bitterly divided into half a dozen rival literary "movements".

Not that Brenner had much faith in what he was doing. On the contrary; just like his wistful characters, and just like his raving opponents, Brenner felt that it was all over and doomed; Zionism and Hebrew, as well as the world of Jewish Eastern Europe. Many of his characters, Tolstoyans who stepped right out of a Dostoievsky novel, were desperate people who maintained that the Jewish people was dying of an incurable, malignant, inherited disease. Nevertheless, something ought to be done in the way of trying to survive and even recover, no matter how pathetic or useless this "something" might be.

Brenner made his characters speak Hebrew; he made them pronounce in it thoughts that were, if anything, existentialist long before existentialism (probably without him knowing the very term "existentialism").

His stories suggest that all of us are left alone in the world and it's up to us to struggle against odds; that we are bound to lose the battle and yet we ought to fight it. Brenner made his lone heroes say all this in Hebrew, perhaps as a kind of metaphysical protest: Hebrew was, after all, the language of the non-existing God; so that a complaint which God would never listen to, let Him not hear it in Hebrew.

It would be unthinkable to call those writers of "The Great Generation" "orthodox" in any sense, but then it would be totally wrong to call them "secular" either. Even the raving atheists among them were obsessed with theology. Even those who denied God along with Judaism altogether were obsessed by the absence of God, and agonized over the stagnation of Judaism. Skeptics like Berdichevsky were nonetheless intrigued by believers. Rebels like Bialik and Brenner were nonetheless writing with a mixture of loathing, anger, and envy about faith and about redemption. Brenner himself even went occasionally so far as creating his own kind of theology for a Godless world.

Brenner, it has been pointed out many times, hated Jews. One Jew he hated in particular — himself. He called his collection of miserable characters, those dropouts, those self-educated little refugees from Eastern Europe, youth without guts or purpose — he called them, "Dead Souls". There are, however, a few stunning exceptions in his stories. But most of them, including even his characters of pioneers in Palestine, where he himself settled in 1909 and where, in 1921, he was murdered by Arab riots; yet most of his characters he described as "Living Ghosts". Hopeless Puritans, endlessly talking of sensual liberation; intellectuals chatting day and night about manual work and about "going back to the land." Little politicians using big words. Eternal wanderers, uprooted forever, exchanging phrases on "roots"; atheists, sweating with guilt and shame whenever they dare to dream about a shadow of a woman. Would-be world reformers who cannot even tie their own shoelaces. Oh, he hated their guts. Yet let me tell you something: with an enemy like Brenner, who needs friends? Brenner's *Breakdown and Bereavement* is available now in English translation; read it and see for yourselves the desperate compassion he had after all for his characters, of whom he sometimes wrote like the worst of all anti-semites. He made them look sick and phony and pompous, or at best pathetic and hopeless. That's what Brenner did, and that is what many other members of "The Great Generation" of modern Hebrew literature did, if not as vehemently. And this, as I'm going to tell you in a few moments, is the real context of even the most contemporary Hebrew literature: the soul-searching, the self-hatred, mingled with compassion, the wrath, the ironies, and a certain sense of "unrealness" about the people, the time, the place, and the language.

Now do you know what actually happened when Brenner's own characters, his own models from real life, read his stories? There happened something which, I believe, is probably unique in the history of world literature: once the characters had read about themselves in the stories by Brenner and his fellow writers, they were deeply hurt, insulted, humiliated, and shocked; in fact they grew very angry; not with Brenner — after all, they had all been through Dostoievsky before — no, they grew angry with themselves and with the entire air of decline and decomposition of Diaspora Jewish life, traditional and "modernized" alike. So Bialik and Berdichevsky and Brenner and the others, without really meaning to, started the fire and the zeal of those few hundreds and eventually thousands of "desperados" who created the foundations for modern Israel. Our grandparents. My own family. In a strange, paradoxical way they burned with desire to show Brenner just how wrong he was. So they stepped right out of his stories and indeed right out of their own skin just to show him that they were not at all what they really were. I realize that this may sound like some wild detective story with characters suddenly leaping out of the pages to demolish their author — but that's how it worked: a literature which was finally meant to commemorate a dying world, ignited a revolution beyond its authors' wildest hopes. And so, eventually, Brenner's own characters made his stories sound wrong and cruel and hateful and shortsighted; his heroes became his refuters. Which is exactly what he might have wished in his heart of hearts.

Now, what has this to do with present-day Israeli literature? When, if ever, am I going to get to the point and talk to you about Zach, Amihai, Pagis, Dahlia Ravikovitch? And what about Appelfeld and Yehoshua and Amalia Cahana-Carmon and their more recent successors?

Apparently, what is happening in the free state of Israel belongs to a brand-new story, in literature and otherwise. Apparently, gone are the days of a ghost language used by desperate writers to mourn a dying world. Can't we just let the dead bury their dead and go about our own business? Indeed, such a mood prevailed over so-called "Sabra Literature" for about one decade, just before and just after independence was achieved. Books seemed to convey a lot of heroism, and to celebrate the Gentile-Jew type, the new heroic, Jewish John Wayne, toiling over the land all day, fighting Arab attackers at dusk, then making wild love to the kibbutz girls all night. There was a combination of glee and macho, perhaps a touch of Hemingway at his worst, and a touch of enthusiastic, Soviet-inspired, Social Realism. But let me stress that even for those euphoric late-forties and fifties, my description is unfair to some major writers and poets like Yizhar, Amir Golboa, and Haim Gury in his better poems. In fact my description refers just to the general widespread literary mood in those years. The pulses of dread and of guilt, of unreality and of neurosis had never disappeared completely from the literary scene.

Since the sixties, roughly, one can decipher a significant revival of themes and tunes and melodies and even techniques which used to be identified with "The Great Generation". It is the basic Hebrew context which reappears in the last two decades: the persistent fear of approaching disaster; time and place which suddenly feel unreal; longings for far-away places; scepticism, irony, and even self-hatred; political siege conceived as emotional siege; persistent, tormented moral-ambiguities; and ultimately the effort, which used to be so typical of "The Great Generation", to sieze within a fluid language a fluid, transitory reality.

The lasting conflict with the Arabs, sixty-five years of bloodshed and five full-scale wars, has not turned our literature into either a patriotic battlecry or else a shallow, whining pacifist manifesto. The conflict has been conceived in Israeli literature as a Greek tragedy, a clash between right and right, rather than as a Wild West film. The sufferings of the Palestinian Arabs are often confronted, in a tragic way, with the historical ordeal of the Jews; Arab fanaticism and ruthlessness is mirrored in several recent novels by the new Israeli arrogance and short-sightedness.

Very much in the footsteps of Brenner and his fellow writers of "The Great Generation", contemporary poets and storytellers tend to fuse the private, personal experience with public, political, and historical dimensions of reality. To many Israelis, history is a biographical experience and biography is soaked with history.

As I was gathering the materials for my recent non-fiction book, *In The Land of Israel*, I was amazed and fascinated to discover to what an extent the person in the street in Israel is obsessed with public affairs; to what an extent the entire Israeli nation is but a passionate seminar on politics, on ideology, on metaphysics, on "the real purpose of God": a fiery collection of arguments, rather than a country or a nation.

In a street cafe in a small town called Bet Shemesh, I found myself surrounded by an angry mob of observant, right-wing, hawkish, Oriental Jews, almost all of them sworn Beginites. They screamed at me that I ought to be hanged, drawn, and quartered for being a secular, a social-democrat, and a dove. Yet those people were showering me with loving kindness and with warm, Oriental hospitality, insisting on paying for my coffee and lighting my cigarettes for me. They treated me as a stray lamb, a confused and embarassing member of their own family. Rather than hang me, they actually strove to save my soul. Which is exactly the way I felt about them; which is exactly what I tried to do with them.

Every line by a bus stop in Israel is likely to catch a spark and turn into a soul-searching, theological session (with its participants, while speculating on "the real significance of Jewish history" and about the secret divine scheme, nonetheless elbowing their way to the front of the line).

If you promise to take it with a grain of salt, I will tell you that this nation of four million citizens is really an uneasy coalition of four million prime ministers, if not four million self-appointed prophets and messiahs.

The current literature reflects this very vividly. You are not likely to find an Israeli novel about an academic writer unable to produce his next book, dashing to see his analyst over this, ending up by writing yet another bloodless novel about an author who went to discuss his writer's block with his analyst. Rather, you will find in our current literature family stories reflecting a general social crisis, or a public crisis becoming the background for a family tale. The political tends to turn metaphysical. An intimate pain begetting a theological quest. A struggle between parent and child reflecting a gap between the magnitude of the initial dreams and visions and the dreariness of petit bourgeois realities. Nostalgia is not the right term here; it is a perpetual yearning for what *could have been*, rather than for any past "finest hour". There is in almost every current work of Israeli literature a secret pulse of messianic yearning.

If there is any common denominator for writers as different from each other as, say, Amihai and Amalia Cahana-Carmon, it is the following: the language strains itself to deal with a gushing river of an unsettled reality. It is still the widespread feeling in today's Israeli literature that whatever looks real and permanent today, has not been there yesterday and might be gone tomorrow; or else that tonight's dreams, nightmares, or horrid memories might become real life next morning.

The Israeli readers do not really enjoy their literature. They read it as if obsessed; they often complain that present-day writers and poets arc dangerous to the ''national morale'' and damaging to Israel's self-image and its reputation in the outside word. So, it may be that one day we, too, are going to irritate our readers to the point of their throwing away our books and cursing us and moving to do something far-fetched and angry about the troubles, old and new.

If and when this happens, it will turn contemporary Israeli literature, even though *post eventum*, into a political literature in the broadest sense of the word. Our readers may then become our refuters. If and when this happens, we may deserve to share the same bookshelf with Brenner and other members of ''The Great Generation''. And finally: you must have seen for yourselves that the story of modern Hebrew has despair and longing, incredible obstinacy along with tremendous will for life. Indeed, it's a story full of sound and fury. Maybe it takes an idiot to try and squeeze some of it into a talk like this.